To my wife Vicki, Mom, Dad, and my Grandmother
Mrs. Dolly Salvato

Thank you for all of your love and support!

**Acknowledgements**

Bob Marlin from Visual Media Inc.
Lynn Marlin from New Horizon Graphics Inc.
David Girgenti from Design Command Center
Steve Johnson from Outsell
Dan Poynter from Para Publishing
René Nedelkoff from Four Colour Imports Ltd.
Ralph Hamm from Friesens

I would also give a special thanks to Robert Thomas, author of "Wall Street Wit and Wisdom" for giving me the inspiration and all the advice he gave me while I was putting this book together. I could not have done it without your help.

Thank you very much.

Introduction

If you are like most people, you know it can be hard to stay motivated and focused 365 days a year whether it be at work, home, school, etc. Especially on those gloomy Monday mornings. Some people listen to their favorite song to get them energized, some read an uplifting story, and others may watch an inspiring movie...the list goes on. I happen to like reading quotes of successful people. I have quotes placed anywhere that I can see them; in my bedroom, my car, and in my office. Sometimes I come into the office and feel a little lethargic and less motivated than I should be in order to do my job effectively. I need something extra besides a cup of strong coffee to get me going. All I do is read a quote from my favorite author or businessman, and I seem to get myself back on track. I put this collection of quotes together to help you do the same. We all have the capabilities to achieve just as much success in life as anyone else. All we need to do is stay motivated and focused, have specific goals and act on them. My hope is that this book gives all of you the extra push you need to get out there and grab life by the horns and achieve all the success life has to offer.

Thomas J. Vilord

What you declare, you will achieve.

To accomplish great things, we must not only act, but also dream, not only plan, but also believe.

– Anatole France

When you think you can't… revisit a previous triumph.

– Jack Canfield

Sometimes things become possible if we want them bad enough.

– T.S. Eliot

To be a leader, you must
stand for something,
or you will fall for anything.

– Anthony Pagano

Don't you get it?
This very second you could be
doing something you love and
dream about doing. So do it!
NOW!

Courage is facing your fears.
Stupidity is fearing nothing.

– Todd Bellemare

The spirit, the will to win,
and the will to excel are the things
that endure. These qualities are so
much more important than the
events that occur.

- Vince Lombardi

Victory is always possible for the
person who refuses to
stop fighting.

– Napoleon Hill

Great works are performed
not by strength,
but perseverance.

– Dr. Samuel Johnson

It doesn't matter what you are
thinking, or what fear you have,
if you just do it! Action is the only
thing that matters…I can see that at
the end of my life, I am not going to
look back and say,
"I wish I had taken more action".
- Diana von Welanetz Wentworth

People become successful the
minute they decide to.

- Harvey Mackay

Winning is not a "sometime" thing. You don't win once in a awhile, you don't do things right once in awhile, you do them right all of the time. Winning is a habit, unfortunately, so is losing.

- Vince Lombardi

Good things come to those who hustle while they wait.

The fastest way to pass your own expectations is to add passion to your labor.

- Mike Litman

Your ideas are like diamonds...without the refining process, they are just a dirty rock, but by cutting away the impurities, they become priceless.

– Paul Kearly

Success is predictable.

– Brian Tracy

To be a champion, you have to
believe in yourself
when nobody else will.

– Sugar Ray Robinson

Time, patience, and perseverance
will accomplish all things.

Society may predict, but only I
can determine my destiny.

– Clair Oliver

Accept the past for what it was. Acknowledge the present for what it is. Anticipate the future for what it can become.
– Tracy L. McNair

To be a winner, all you have to give is all you have.

Successful people tend to become more successful because they are always thinking about their successes.
– Brian Tracy

If we are to achieve results never before accomplished, we must expect to employ methods never before attempted.
– Francis Bacon

I have tried 99 times and have failed, but on the 100th time came success.
— Albert Einstein

Success is more attitude than aptitude.

Our mind is the most valuable possession that we have. The quality of our lives is, and will be, a reflection of how well we develop, train, and utilize this precious gift.
— Brian Tracy

The past is over…forget it. The future holds hope…reach for it.

— Charles R. Swindoll

There is always a better way.

– Thomas Edison

Having conceived of his purpose, a man should mentally mark out a straight pathway to its achievement, looking neither to the right or to the left, but straight.

– James Allen

The habit of persistence is the habit of victory.

– Herbert Kaufman

People with goals succeed because they know where they are going.

– Earl Nightingale

For I can do ALL things through Christ who gives me strength.

– Philippians 4:13

Excellence is not being the best; it is doing your best.

When everything feels like an uphill struggle, just think of the view from the top.

To me, a winner is someone who recognizes their God-given talents, works his tail off to develop them into skills, and uses those skills to accomplish his goals. Even when I lost, I learned what my weaknesses were and I went out the next day to turn those weaknesses into strengths.

– Larry Bird

The size of your success depends on the depth of your desire.

Don't limit your challenges; challenge your limits.

Each day we must strive for constant and never ending improvement.

– Anthony Robbins

If you have a burning desire and a plan to take action, there is absolutely nothing you cannot achieve.

– Thomas J. Vilord

Approach the start of each day with something in mind and end the day with one word...DONE.

Dreamers look into the future and see promise. Those who do not dream only see the future.

– D. Elder

Life is only what we choose to make it.

Happiness is the highest level of success.

In every problem there is a
hidden treasure inside.
It's your job to find it.

Fear is met and destroyed with
courage. Again and again when the
struggle seems hopeless and all
opportunity lost, the one with a
little more courage, and a little more
effort will have victory.

– James F. Bell

Anyone who has never made a
mistake has never tried anything
new.

– Albert Einstien

Without ambition no conquests
are made, and no business created.
Ambition is the root of all
achievement.

– James Champy

Cause change and lead;
accept change and survive;
resist change and die.

— Ray Norda

80% of success is showing up.

— Woody Allen

To change bad habits, we must
study the habits of successful role
models.

— Jack Canfield

He who dares, wins.

— Winston Churchill

Trust in yourself. Your perceptions are often far more accurate than you are willing to believe.

– Claudia Black

Imagination rules the world.

– Napoleon Bonaparte

If you think you can or if you think you can't, either way you are right.

– Anthony Robbins

God created all men equal. Why do some accomplish far greater accomplishments then others? Because they had a vision, a desire, and they took action.

– Thomas J. Vilord

We can do anything we want to if we stick to it long enough.

– Helen Keller

Some men give up their designs when they have almost reached their goal, while others obtain a victory by exerting, at the last moment, more vigorous efforts than ever before.

– Herodotus

Motivation is like food for the brain. You cannot get enough in one sitting. It needs continual and regular refills.

– Peter Davies

Only those who risk going too far can possibly find out how far one can go.

– T.S. Eliot

The achievement of one goal should be the starting point of another.

– Alexander Graham Bell

Concentrated thoughts produce desired results.

– Zig Ziglar

People are anxious to improve their circumstances, but are unwilling to improve themselves. That is why they remain bound.

– James Allen

Genius is divine perseverance. Genius I cannot have, but perseverance all can have.

– Woodrow Wilson

Money never starts an idea; it's the idea that starts the money.

- Mark Victor Hansen

I am not just here to make a living; I am here to make a life.

– Helice Bridges

Life is short. Focus from this day forward on making a difference.

Ideas are a dime a dozen, they are worthless, but people who put their ideas into action are priceless.

You may be disappointed if you fail, but you are doomed if you do not try.
– Beverly Sills

It's not whether you get knocked down; it's whether you get back up.
– Vince Lombardi

Success is the prize for those who stand true to their ideas.

– John S. Hinds

I would rather fail in a cause that would ultimately succeed, than succeed in a cause that would ultimately fail.
– Woodrow Wilson

Success is neither magical nor mysterious. Success is the natural consequence of consistently applying the basic fundamentals.
- Jim Rohn

The path to success is to take massive determined action.

– Anthony Robbins

I know the price of success: dedication, hard work, and an unremitting devotion to the things you want to see happen.
-Frank Lloyd Wright

Your dreams minus your doubts equal your true worth.

The man who said he never had a chance, never took one.

Dream your wildest dreams and you will live a wild life.

Success comes to those who dare to begin.

Your success is only limited by your desire.

I have failed over and over again. That is why I succeed.

– Michael Jordan

Read something positive every night and listen to something helpful every morning.

– Tom Hopkins

Never stop learning. If you learn one new thing everyday, you will overcome 99% of your competition.

– Joe Carlozo

Winning doesn't make you a better person, but being a better person will make you a winner.

I do believe I am special. My special gift is my vision, my commitment, and my willingness to do whatever it takes.
– Anthony Robbins

The starting point of all achievement is desire. Keep this constantly in mind. Weak desire brings weak results, just as a small amount of fire makes a small amount of heat.
– Napoleon Hill

Man is what he believes.

– Anton Chekov

It is the mind that makes good or ill. That which makes us happy or sad; rich or poor.

– Edmund Spencer

It's a funny thing about life; if you refuse to accept anything but the best, you often get it.

– W. Somerset Manghan

With each choice you make, you create your life.

Never give up! Failure and rejection are only the first step to succeeding.

– Jimmy Valvano

Believe in yourself and you will be unstoppable.

– Emily Guay

Failure is merely part of the process necessary for success.

The door to success is the one marked PUSH.

There are no failures in life, only those who give up to soon.

Don't wish for it...work for it!

He who conquers others is strong.
He who conquers himself is
mighty.

– Lao Tzu

Don't be afraid to go after what
you want to do and what you want
to be, and don't be afraid to pay
the price to get it.

The best way to accomplish
something is to just do it, and
then find the courage afterwards.

JUST DO IT! – Nike

Never let your fears be the boundaries of your dreams.

Think BIG! You are going to be thinking anyway, so think BIG!

– Donald Trump

We grow great by dreams. All big men are dreamers. They see things in the soft haze of a spring day or in the red fire of a long winters evening. Some of us let these great dreams die, but others nourish and protect them; they nurse them through bad days until they bring them to the sunshine and the light that always comes to those who sincerely hope that their dreams will come true.

– Woodrow Wilson

Success in the end erases all the mistakes along the way.

— Chinese Proverb

Success is a piece of mind which is a direct result of the self-satisfaction knowing you did your best to become the best you are capable of becoming.

— John Wooden

Life's battles don't always go to the faster, stronger man. The man who wins is the man who thinks he can.

People become really quite remarkable when they start thinking that they can do things. When they believe in themselves, they have the first secret of success.

— Norman Vincent Peale

The day I stop giving is the day I stop receiving. The day I stop learning is the day I stop growing.

Winners are ordinary people with extraordinary heart.

The only difference between dreams and achievements is hard work.

– Mayor Chris Bollwage.

The happiest of people do not necessarily have the best of everything. They just make the most of everything that comes along their way.

True success in life is not measured by how much you make, but by how much of a difference you make.

Allow yourself to dream and fantasize about your ideal life; what it would look like, and what it would feel like. Then do something everyday to make it a reality!

— Brian Tracy

The secret of success is consistency of purpose.

— Benjamin Disraeli

If the mind of man can believe, the mind of man can achieve.

— Napoleon Hill

To conquer without risk is to triumph without glory.

– El Cid

Thoughts and ideas are the source of all wealth, success, material gain, all great discoveries, inventions and achievements.

– Mark Victor Hansen

You miss 100% of the shots you don't take.

– Wayne Gretzky

I am not judged by the number of times I fail, but the number of times I succeed, and the number of times I succeed is a direct proportion to the number of times I fail and keep trying.

– Tom Hopkins

No man ever became great without many and great mistakes.

– William E. Gladstone

Add value to everyday. Sharpen your skills and your understanding.

People of mediocre ability sometimes achieve outstanding success because they don't know when to quit. Most men succeed because they are determined to.

– George E. Allen

Life is filled with possibilities.

Decide what is worthwhile and follow through with it.

I do not think there is any other quality so essential to success of any kind as the quality of perseverance. It overcomes almost everything, even nature.
– John D. Rockefeller

Real success is finding your life work in the work that you love.

– David McCullough

Creativity means believing you have greatness.

– Dr. Wayne D. Dwyer

I can't believe that God put us on this earth just to be ordinary.

– Lou Holtz

Believe that you have it, and you will have it.

– Latin Proverb

In the long run, we only hit what we aim at.

– Henry David Thoreau

Start each day by affirming peaceful, contented, and happy attitudes and your days will tend to be pleasant and successful.

– Norman Vincent Peale

There is no shortcut.
Victory lies in overcoming
obstacles everyday.

The key to achievement is
being a How thinker and
not an If thinker.

If I had to select one quality and
one personal characteristic that I
regard as being most highly
correlated with success, whatever
the field, I would pick persistence
and determination. The will to
endure to the end, to get knocked
down seventy times and
get up off the floor saying,
"Here comes number seventy one".

– Richard M. Devos

The happiest life is that which consistently exercises and educates what is best in us.

– Philip G. Hamerton

Our aspirations are our possibilities.

– Samuel Johnson

Innovate, develop, motivate, inspire, trust - be a leader.

There is nothing training cannot do. Nothing is above its reach. It can turn bad morals to good morals; it can destroy bad principles and re-create good ones; it can lift men to angelship.

– Mark Twain

Discovery lies in seeing what everyone sees, but thinking what know one has thought.

Be courageous! Have faith! Go forward.

– Thomas A. Edison

Life is built of the things we do. The only constructive material is positive action.

The actual is limited, the possibilities immense.

– LaMartine

Success seems to be connected with action. Successful men keep moving; they make mistakes, but they do not quit.
– Conrad Hilton

Do not settle for less than an extraordinary life.

Success is not always achieved by hard work alone, but mix it with a little bit of organization and a little strength from God above and you'll have a winning recipe.

You have to find something that you love enough to be able to take risks, jump over the hurdles and break though the brick walls that are always going to be placed in front of you. If you don't have that kind of feeling for what it is you are doing, you'll stop at the first giant hurdle.
- George Lucas

Stay focused and stay curious. Do what you say you will do.

Always keep a window open in your mind for new ideas.

I maintained my edge by always being a student; you will always have something new to learn.

– Jackie Joyner Kersee

Keys to success: Research your ideas, plan for success, expect success, and just do it.

– John S. Hinds

This is America...we can do anything here!

– Ted Turner

I am a great believer in luck, and I find that the harder I work the more luck I have.

– Thomas Jefferson

You've got to get up every morning with determination if you're going to go to bed with satisfaction.

– George Horace Lorimer

Destiny is not a matter of chance; it's a matter of choice. It is not a thing to be waited for; it is a thing to be achieved.

– Jeremy Kitson

Every success is built on the ability to do better than good enough.

If you want your life to be a magnificent story, then begin by realizing that you are the author and everyday you have the opportunity to write a new page.

– Mark Houlahan

Nothing great was ever achieved without enthusiasm.

– Ralph Waldo Emerson

Why? Why not? Why not you? Why not now?

– Aslan

Consult not your fears, but your hopes and your dreams. Think not about your frustrations, but about your unfilled potential. Concern yourself not with what you have tried and failed in, but for what is still possible for you to do.

- Pope John XXIII

What lies behind us and what lies before us are tiny matters compared to what lies within us.

– Ralph Waldo Emerson

In life, those that are great are those that dare to follow their dreams through the good times AND the bad times.

Out of difficulties grow miracles.

– Jean De La Bruyere

We must all suffer one of two things: The pain of discipline or the pain of regret and disappointment.

– Jim Rohn

Faith is to believe what you do not yet see; the reward for this faith is to see what you believe.

– St. Augustine

If I have the belief that I can do it, I shall surely acquire the capacity to do it even if I may not have the capacity at the beginning.

– Mahatma Ghandi

The greatest glory in living lies not in never falling, but in rising every time we fall.

– Nelson Mandela

All of our dreams can come true if we have the courage to pursue them.

– Walt Disney

Through perseverance, many people win success out of what seemed destined to be certain failure.

– Benjamin Disraeli

To succeed, you need to take that gut feeling in what you believe and act on it with all of your heart.

– Christy Borgeld

Believe in a hope that a new hope is dawning...believe that your dreams will come true...believe in the promise of brighter tomorrows...begin by believing in you.

Reach for the moon.
If you fall short at least
you'll be among the stars.

It's in your moments of decision
that your destiny is shaped.

– Anthony Robbins

Focus on where you want to go,
not where your currently are.

If you can't do it today, what
makes you think you can do it
tomorrow.

– Yusuf Tara

The only thing you have to fear is not giving 100%.

To be successful you must decide exactly what you want to accomplish, and then resolve to pay the price to get it.

— Bunker Hunt

There are no limitations to any of our dreams.

— Gene Simmons

Believe...and the magic will follow.

Success is not where you are in life, but the obstacles you have overcome.

– Booker T. Washington

Life is an adventure! Live it while you can. You can never have today again, tomorrow only comes once, and yesterday is gone forever. Make your choice wisely, then live the adventure you create.

Action may not bring happiness, but there is no happiness without action.

– William James

Our intentions create our reality.

– Dr. Wayne W. Dyer

We cannot always control what goes on outside, but we can control what goes on inside.

Some men have thousands of reasons why they cannot do what they want to; all they need is one reason why they can.

– Willis Whitney

There are essentially two things that will make us wiser: the books we read and the people we meet.

– Charles Jones

If you realized how powerful your thoughts are, you would never think another negative thought.

– Peace Pilgrim

Experience tells you what to do. Confidence allows you to do it.

– Stan Smith

Everything you want is on the other side of fear.

– Jack Canfield

If there is something to gain and nothing to lose by asking, by all means ask!

– W. Clement Stone

If you consistently and persistently do the things that other successful people do, nothing in the world can stop you from being a big success also.

– Brian Tracy

Your ability will grow to match your dreams.

– Jim Rohn

I know of no more encouraging fact than the unquestionable ability of man to elevate his life by conscious effort.

– Henry David Thoreau

Ask yourself, "Am I now ready to make some changes."

– Jack Canfield

Keep going, for success lies just around the corner for those who refuse to quit.

Ask for the business…always!

The majority of men meet with failure because of their lack of persistence in creating new plans to take the place of those that fail.
– Napoleon Hill

Things that matter most must never be at the mercy of things that matter least.

– Johann Wolfgang von Goethe

Your income rarely exceeds your personal development.

– Jim Rohn

You are the architect of your own destiny; you are the master of your own fate; you are behind the steering wheel of your life. There are no limitations to what you can do, have, or be. Accept the limitations you place on yourself by your own thinking.
— Brian Tracy

Your habits will determine your quality of life.

You must learn from your past mistakes, but not lean on your past successes.

— Denis Waitley

It's so hard when contemplated in advance, and so easy when you just do it.
— Robert M. Pirsig
(about forming positive habits)

All leaders are readers.

– Jim Rohn

You can turn negative consequences into positive rewards simply by changing your habits now.

The individual who wants to reach the top in business must appreciate the mighty force of habit and must understand that practices are what create habits. We must be quick to break those old habits that break us and hasten to adopt those practices that will become the habits that will help us achieve the success we desire.

– J. Paul Getty

Somebody is always doing what somebody else said couldn't be done.

The one thing that separates the winners from the losers, is, winners take action.

– Anthony Robbins

If you have goals and procrastination you have nothing. If you have goals and you take action, you will have anything you want.

– Thomas J. Vilord

Every well-built house started with a definite plan in the form of blueprints.

– Napoleon Hill (on setting goals)

Remember, if you want a different result, do something different.

A brilliant idea without action is like Mark McGwire playing baseball without a bat.

– Jack Canfield

Quality is not an act - it is a habit.

The life that is not examined is not worth living.

– Socrates

Develop the habit of changing your habits.

One can dream of horizons bigger than the imagination – how you go about implementing those dreams will be the key to your success.

Everyday is a gift, that is why it is called the present.

It is not what you say or hope, wish or intend, but only what you do that counts. Your choices tell you unerringly who you really are.

– Brian Tracy

Happiness is not getting what you want, but wanting what you've got.

Man alone has the power to transfer his thoughts into physical reality; man alone can dream and make his dreams come true.

– Napoleon Hill

Success never comes to look for you while you wait around. You've got to get up and work at it to make your dreams come true.

– Poh Yu Khing

Commit yourself to life long learning. The most valuable asset you will ever have is your mind and what you put into it.

– Brian Tracy

If I can dream, I can act and if I can act, I can become.

– Poh Yu Khing

On the path to success always lies big O's. Some read them as Obstacles, and others read them as Opportunities.

Success is committing to give your best no matter what the circumstances.

There are no losers in losing, only losers in not wanting to win.

– Jesus M. Trejo

To the world you may be one person, but to one person you may be the world.

– Paulette Mitchell

A time comes when you need to stop waiting for the man you want to become and start being the man you want to be.

– Bruce Springsteen

What have you done today to help you reach your lifelong goals?

– Brian Tracy

A dream is not something that you wake up from, but something that wakes you up.

– Charlie Hedges

The only way to discover the limits of the possible is to go beyond them into the impossible.

– Arthur C. Clark

If we always look back, we lose sight of what's ahead.

– Justin Sims

Believe you will be successful and you will.

– Dale Carnegie

You cannot have everything, but you can try.

Success is measured in terms of reaching your goals, dreams, and expectations. Your success is determined by hard work, persistence, and determination. If you are going to be a success in life it's all up to you....it's your responsibility.
— Will Horton

You can never dream too big, but you can think too little.

If you can dream it and you want it bad enough, then the reality will become real.

The toughest part of working up the ladder is fighting through the crowd at the bottom.

A man has two names: the one he is born with and the one that he makes for himself.

If at first you don't succeed, dust yourself off and try again.

– Aaliyah (song lyrics)

Sometimes a winner is just a dreamer that never gave up.

You are what you repeatedly do. Excellence is not an event – it is a habit.

- Aristotle

Success comes from having dreams that are bigger than your fears.

– Terry Litwiller

I'd rather attempt to do great things and blow it, than succeed at meaningless things and just get by.

Hope doesn't guarantee anything – hard work does.

I feel the most important requirement to success is learning to overcome failure. You must learn to tolerate it, but never accept it.

– Reggie Jackson

Spectacular achievement is always preceded by painstaking preparation.

– Roger Staubach

Some things have to be believed to be seen.

– Ralph Hodgson

Man is not the creature of circumstances; circumstances are the creatures of man.

– Benjamin Disraeli

I am not discouraged, because every wrong attempt discarded is another step forward.

– Thomas Edison

We will either find a way or make one.

– Hannibal

The secret of success is learning how to use pain and pleasure instead of having pain and pleasure use you. If you do that, you are in control of your life. If you don't, life controls you.

– Anthony Robbins

Money itself won't bring happiness, but it sure makes paying the bills easier.

– Thomas J. Vilord

Things do not change – we change.

– Henry David Thoreau

Ask and you will receive, seek and you will find, knock and the door will be opened to you.

– Matthew 7:7

Nothing happens unless first a dream.

– Carl Sandberg

Take a risk - jump out of your comfort zone!

Don't let self-doubt hold you back!

Overcome fear by taking action!

Successful people in this world are those who get up and look for circumstances they want. If you can't find them, then make them.
– George Bernard Shaw

Enthusiasm creates action.

Where there is no vision, people perish.

– Proverbs 29:18

Habit is either the best of servants or the worst of masters.

– Nathaniel Emmons

Hold yourself to a higher standard than anybody else expects of you.

– Henry Ward Beecher

We lift ourselves by our thoughts. We climb upon our vision of ourselves.

– Orison Swett Marden

Imagination is more important than knowledge.

– Albert Einstein

I think, therefore I am.

– Rene Descartes

The price of excellence is discipline. The cost of mediocrity is disappointment.

– William W. Ward

If we did all of the things we are capable of doing, we would literally astound ourselves.

– Thomas A. Edison

Wealth is the product of a man's ability to think.

– Ayn Rand

Every man is an impossibility until he is born.

– Ralph Waldo Emerson

Only those who have learned the power of sincere and selfless contribution will ever experience life's deepest joy; true fulfillment.

– Anthony Robbins

The history of the world is the history of a few men who had faith in themselves. That faith calls out the divinity within. You can do anything!

– Swami Vivekananda

Success is having your best day everyday.

The only difference between success and failure is the ability to take action.

– Alexander Grahm Bell

A powerful combination to ensure success is having the vision of an eagle and the heart of a lion.

The average person puts about 25% of his energy and ability into his work. The world takes its hat off to those who put more than 50% of their capacity into their work, and the world stands on its head for those few and far between souls who devote 100%.

– Andrew Carnegie

Fear begins to melt away when you begin to take action on a goal you really want.

– Robert G. Allen

Action must be taken at once! There is no time to be lost.

— Miguel Hidalgo

The greater the obstacle, the more glory in achieving it.

— Moliere

Ideas shape the course of history.

— John Keynes

To move the world, we must first move ourselves.

— Socrates

It takes time to be a success, but time is all it takes.

Where are you going? What are you doing today to get there?

We must never be afraid to go too far, for success lies just beyond.

– Marcel Proust

You see things and say "Why?" but I dream of things that never were and say "Why not?"

– George Bernard Shaw

They can because they
think they can.

– Virgil

People are not lazy; they just have
impotent goals, that is, goals that
do not inspire them.

– Anthony Robbins

Nothing is possible if you think it
is impossible. Nothing is
impossible if you think it is
possible. Think positive and work
hard, and ANYTHING is possible.
– Thomas J. Vilord

Winning starts with beginning.

Anything that enlarges the sphere of human powers and shows man he can do what he thought he could not do is valuable.
— Ben Johnson

If you do what you've always done, you'll get what you've always gotten.

That which is achieved the most, still has the whole of it's future yet to be achieved.

- Lao Tsu

Man is not the sum of what he has, but the totality of what he does not yet have and what he might have.
— Jean Paul Sartre

The great end of life is not knowledge, but action.

– Thomas Henry Huxley

Have a dream so BIG that you cannot achieve it until you grow into the person who can.

Success is neither a high jump nor a long jump; it is the steps of a marathon.

If opportunity doesn't knock, build a door.

Take up one idea and act on it. Make that one idea your life. Think of it, dream of it, and live on that idea. Let the brain, muscles, nerves, and every part of your body be full of that idea and leave all other ideas alone. This is the way to success.

If you have failed, do not worry. You have just cut the way to success.

Failure is never as scary as regret.

Successful people do what unsuccessful people dare not to.

Anything you vividly imagine, ardently desire, sincerely believe, and enthusiastically act upon must come to reality.

Without a goal, discipline is nothing but self-punishment.

It is not enough to have knowledge; one must apply it. It is not enough to have wishes; one must also accomplish it.

– Johann Wolfgang von Goethe

Never let a day pass that will make you say, "I will do better tomorrow".

Become a possibilitarian. No matter how dark things seem to be or actually are, raise your sights and see the possibilities – always see them, for they are always there.

– Norman Vincent Peale

The word can't is not in the successful man's vocabulary.

Real success is not having things, but having victory over yourself.

I haven't failed; I have just found 10,000 ways that didn't work.

– Thomas A. Edison

Failure doesn't mean that we are off the track to success. It merely forces us to take a detour to success.

Tomorrow is now.

– Elanor Roosevelt

If your life is free of failures, you are not taking enough risks.

The secret to success is to be ready when opportunity comes.

– Benjamin Disraeli

Do extraordinary things; don't just dream them.

Exceed expectations. We are not driven to do extraordinary things, but to do ordinary things extraordinarily well.
– Bishop Gore

Practice is just as valuable as a sale. The sale will make you a living; the skill will make you a fortune.
– Jim Rohn

Show me someone who has done something worthwhile, and I'll show you someone who has overcome adversity.
– Lou Holtz

Success is peace of mind, which is a direct result of self-satisfaction in knowing that you did your best to become the best you are capable of becoming.
– John Wooden

The world makes way for a man who knows where he is going.

– Ralph Waldo Emerson

Our limitations and success will be based most often on our own expectations for ourselves. What the mind dwells upon, the body acts upon.
– Thomas Dewar

You may have a fresh start at any moment you choose, for this thing we call "failure" is not falling down, but staying down.
– Mary Pickford

We must walk consciously only part way toward our goal, and then leap into the dark to our success.
– Henry David Thoreau

Step by step. I can't think of any other way of accomplishing anything.

– Michael Jordan

Plan your work for today and everyday, and then work on your plan today and everyday.

– Norman Vincent Peale

The only limit of our realization of tomorrow will be our doubts of today.

– Franklin D. Roosevelt

The pessimist sees difficulty in every opportunity; an optimist sees the opportunity in every difficulty.

— Winston Churchill

To win, you have to risk loss.

— Jean Claude Killy

High expectations are the key to everything.

— Sam Walton

The victory of success is half won when one gains the habit of setting goals and achieving them. Even the most tedious chore will become endurable as you parade through each day convinced that every task, no matter how menial or boring, brings you closer to achieving your dreams.

- Og Mandino

The only place success comes before work is in the dictionary.

– Donald Kendall

It takes the hammer of persistence to drive the nail of success.

– John Mason

It is not the mountain we conquer, but ourselves.

– Sir Edmund Hillary

Entrepreneurs are simply those who understand that there is little difference between obstacle and opportunity, and are able to turn both to their advantage.

– Victor Kiam

The quality of a person's life is in direct proportion to their commitment to excellence, regardless of their chosen field of endeavor.

– Vince Lombardi

He who stops being better, stops being good.

– Oliver Cromwell

Once you learn to quit it becomes a habit.

It is what you learn after you know it all that counts.

– John Wooden

If what you did yesterday seems big, you haven't done anything today.

– Lou Holtz

He who asks a question is a fool for five minutes. He who does not ask a question is a fool forever.

Every great and commanding movement in the annals of the world is the triumph of enthusiasm. Nothing great was ever achieved without it.
– Ralph Waldo Emerson

It is the constant and determined effort that breaks down resistance and sweeps away all obstacles.

– Claude M. Bristol

Every failure is a step to success.

Commit yourself to a dream. Nobody who tries to do something great, but fails, is a total failure. Why? Because he can always be assured that he succeeded in life's most important battle; he defeated the battle of not trying.
— Robert H. Schuller

Always do your best. What you plant now, you will harvest later.

— Og Mandino

Predetermine the objectives that you want to accomplish. Think big, act big, and set out to accomplish big results!

— Mark Victor Hansen

Courage is not the absence of fear, but rather the judgment that something else is more important than one's fear.

– Ambrose Redmoon

In reading the lives of great men, I found that the first victory they won were over themselves… self-discipline with all of them came first.

– Harry S. Truman

The men who succeed are the efficient few. They are the few who have the ambition and will power to develop themselves.

– Herbert N. Casson

The difference between the impossible and the possible lies in a man's determination.

– Tommy Lasorda

Most of our obstacles would melt away if, instead of cowering before them, we should make up our minds to walk boldly through them.
– Orison Swett Marden

Obstacles are those frightful things you see when you take your eyes off you goal.

– Henry Ford

The fight is won or lost far away from witnesses – behind the lines, in the gym, and out there on the road, long before I dance under those lights.
– Muhammed Ali

The man who says it cannot be done should not interrupt the man doing it.

– Chinese Proverb

Failure is good. It is fertilizer. Everything I have learned about coaching, I have learned from making mistakes.
— Rick Petino

Victory belongs to the most persevering.

— Napoleon Bonaparte

The ultimate measure of a man is not where he stands in moments of comfort and convenience, but where he stands at times of challenges and controversy.
— Dr. Martin Luther King, Jr.

The person who goes the farthest is generally the one who is willing to do and dare. The "sure thing" boat never gets offshore.
- Dale Carnegie

If you can dream it, you can do it.

- Walt Disney

In each of us there are places we have never gone. Only by pressing the limits do you ever find them.

– Dr. Joyce Brothers

Man is so made that when anything fires his goal, impossibilities vanish!

- Jean De La Fountaine

Picture in your mind a sense of personal destiny!

Twenty years from now you will be more disappointed by the things you didn't do, then by the things you did do. So throw off the bowlines! Sail away from the safe harbor. Catch the trade winds in your sails. Explore, dream, and discover.

- Mark Twain

A dream is just a dream. A goal is a dream with a plan and a deadline.

- Harvey Mackay

Enthusiasm finds the opportunities, and energy makes the most of them.

-Henry Hoskins

It is good to dream, but it is better to dream and work. Faith is mighty, but faith with action is mightier. Desiring is helpful, but desire and work is invincible.

- Thomas Robert Gaines

Many people dream of success. To me success can only be achieved through repeated failure and introspection.
- Soichiro Honda

People become really quite remarkable when they start thinking that they can do things. When they believe in themselves they have the first secret of success.
- Norman Vincent Peale

Real leaders are ordinary people with extraordinary determination.

The future belongs to those who believe in their dreams.

We do not know who we are until we see what we can do.

- Martha Grimes

Continuous effort! not strength or intelligence, is the key to unlocking your potential.

- Winston Churchill

Your dreams come true when you act to turn them into realities.

Life without risk is not worth living.

- Charles Lindbergh

Opportunities are usually disguised by hard work, so most people don't recognize them.

- Ann Landers

Don't be afraid of the space between your dreams and reality. If you can dream it, you can make it so.

- Belva Davis

You don't have to be a fantastic hero to do certain things to compete. You can just be an ordinary person, sufficiently motivated to reach challenging goals.
– Sir Edmund Hillary

If you proclaim it and believe it, you will absolutely achieve it.

Luck is when preparedness meets opportunity.

- Earl Nightingale

When you get into a tight place and everything goes against you, until it seems as though you could not hang on a minute longer, it is then when you should never give up, for that is just the place and time when the tide will turn.

- Harriet Beecher Stowe

It takes no more effort to expect the best, than to fear for the worst. It's healthier, more productive, and a lot more fun.

- Philip E. Hambert, Ph.D.

Begin somewhere; you can't build a reputation on what you intend to do.

- Liz Smith

It had long since come to my attention that people of accomplishment rarely sat back and let things happen to them. They went out and made things happen.

- Elinor Smith

We cannot discover new oceans until we have the courage to lose sight of the shore.

- Muriel Chen

Dreams are renewable. No matter what our age or condition, there are still untapped possibilities within us, and a new beauty waiting to be born.

- Dr. Dale Turner

The best way to predict your future is to create it.

Hope sees the invisible, feels the intangible, and achieves the impossible.

- Charles Caleb Colton

It is our duty as men and women to proceed as though the limits of our abilities do not exist.

- Pierre Teilhard de Chardin

Life begets life. Energy creates energy. It is by spending oneself that one becomes rich.

- Sarah Bernhardt

Living never wore one out so much as the effort not to live.

- Anais Nin

It seems to me that we can never give up longing and wishing while we are alive. There are certain things we feel to be beautiful and good, and we must hunger for them always.

- George Eliot

Effort equals results.

Sometimes life may seem like a tunnel, endless and dark, but don't concentrate on the darkness. Concentrate on the light at the end, and you will succeed.

Do your work with your whole heart, and you will succeed because there is so little competition.

- Elbert Hubbard

Men of genius are admired, men of wealth are envied, men of power are feared, but only men of character are trusted.
- Zig Ziglar

If you are not happy every morning when you get up, leave for work, or start to work at home, and are not enthusiastic about doing that, you will not be successful.
- Donald M. Kendall

You can change the way you feel by changing the way you think.

When you believe in yourself and dream big, anything is possible.

Strength does not come from winning. Your struggles develop your strength. When you go through hardship and decide not to surrender, that is strength.
- Arnold Schwarzenegger

If you want your dreams to come true then WAKE UP!

If you continue to work hard, success will follow you.

Success is to stand in the presence of God unashamed.

Success is not the position you stand, but the direction in which you look.

If you always do what you've always done, you'll always be what you are now.

A habit is like a cable: we weave a thread of it everyday, and at last we cannot break it - so we must form good, positive, and productive habits.
- Horace Mann

Life is too short to ponder the "what if's" and fear rejection.

– T. Dufek

What is fear? F= false, E= evidence, A= appearing, R= real. Don't be afraid of any false evidence and just do it.

To be number one, you have to train like you are number two.

Live your imagination, not your history.

— Stephen Covy

Without continuous personal development, you are now all that you will ever become, and hell starts when the person you are meets the person you could have been.

— Eli Cohen

Ambition is success's best friend.

There is only one way to fail and that is to quit.

Don't let your success of today lay you into complacency for tomorrow. For that is the worst form of failure.

– Og Mandino

If you want to win, go and meet those who lost.

You can get everything you want
if you help enough others
get what they want.

– Zig Ziglar

It is no sin to attempt and fail.
The only sin is to not make
the attempt.

– Suellen Fried

Your current conditions do not
reflect your ultimate potential.

- Anthony Robbins

When you think big,
your results are big.

– Thomas J. Vilord

Life is change; growth is optional. Choose wisely.

– Karen Kaiser Clark

Everything changes when you change.

– Jim Rohn

You don't have to be great to get started, but you have to get started to be great.

– Les Brown

The key to unlocking my potential is within me. It is the power of my thought, my vision, and my commitment!

Living itself is a risky business. If we spent half as much time learning how to take risks as we spend avoiding them, we wouldn't have so much fear in life.

— E. Paul Torrance

I will…until.

— Brian Tracy

The best way to cheer yourself up is to cheer everybody else up.

— Mark Twain

The law of cause and effect: If you do what other successful people do, you will eventually get the results that other successful people get.

— Brian Tracy

Dream big dreams. Only big dreams have the power to move men's souls.

– Marais Aurelius

A person with a clear purpose will make progress on even the roughest road. A person with no purpose will make no progress even on the smoothest road.

– Thomas Carlyle

I am the captain of my soul. I am the master of my fate.

– William Henley

When you start doing what you love to do, you will never work another day in your life.

– Brian Tracy

The harder I work,
the luckier I get.

– James Thurber

Continuous learning is the
minimum requirement for
success in any field!

– Denis Waitley

Thought is the original source of
all wealth, all success, all material
gain, all great discoveries and
inventions, and all achievement.

– Claude M. Bristol

Self-discipline is the ability
to make yourself do what you
should do, when you should do it,
whether you feel like it or not.

– Elbert Hubbard

Nothing can take the place of persistence. Talent will not; nothing is more common than unsuccessful men with talent. Genius will not; unrewarded genius is almost a proverb. Education will not; the world is full of educated derelicts. Persistence and determination alone are omnipotent.

– Calvin Coolidge

We need men who can dream of things that never were.

– John F. Kennedy

I must create a system, or be enslaved in another man's. I will not reason and compare; my business is to create.

– William Blake

The principle of competing is against yourself. It's about self-improvement, and being better than you were the day before.

– Steve Young

In the middle of difficulty lies opportunity.

– Albert Einstein

Nurture the dreams that will inspire you to go beyond your limits.

The mind quickly responds to teaching and discipline. You can make the mind give you back anything you want.

– Norman Vincent Peale

Achievement comes when you decide to live your possibilities!

If you want to double your success rate, you need to double your failure rate.

– Thomas John Watson, Sr.

Excellence is attained when you care more than others think is wise; risk more than others think is safe; dream more than others think is practical; expect more than others think is possible.

– Jim Gentil

Don't think problem, think opportunity.

If you worry about yesterday's failures, then today's successes will be few.

The history of the human race is the history of ordinary people who have overcome their fears and have accomplished extraordinary things.

– Brian Tracy

Success could be described as 50/50 – 50% vision and 50% action.

Dreams are the reality of tomorrow.

– Dean Marshall

Get enthusiastic and excited about your dreams. This excitement is like a forest fire – you can smell it, taste it, and see it from a mile away.

– Denis Waitley

There will never be another now.
I will make the most of today.
There will never be another me.
I will make the most of myself.

– Robert H. Schuller

The man who can drive himself
farther once the effort gets painful,
is the man who will win.

– Roger Bannister

What this power is I cannot
say. All I know is that it exists and it
becomes available only when a man
is in that state of mind in which he
knows exactly what he wants and is
fully determined not to quit until
he finds it.
– Alexander Grahm Bell

Every worthwhile
accomplishment, big or little, has
its stages of drudgery and
triumph; a beginning, a struggle,
and a victory.

– Ghandi

The only good luck many great men ever had was being born with the ability and determination to overcome bad luck.

– Channing Pollock

Obstacles don't have to stop you. If you run into a wall, don't turn around and give up. Figure out how to climb it, go through it, or work around it.

– Michael Jordan

Knowing is not enough;
we must apply.
Willing is not enough;
we must do.

- Johann Wolfgang von Goethe

You can't leave footprints in the sands of time if you are sitting on you butt, and who wants to leave buttprints in the sands of time!

– Bob Moawad

Relentlessness and discontent are the first necessities of progress.

– Thomas A. Edison

First say to yourself what you would be, then do what you have to do.

– Epictetus

Be all that you can be.

– ARMY slogan

There is no achievement without goals.

– Robert J. McKaine

Don't start the day until you have it finished. Don't start the week until you have it finished. Don't start the month until you have it finished. Plan your day.

– Jim Rohn

Never let the fear of striking out get in your way.

– Babe Ruth

Be absolutely determined to enjoy what you do.

– Gerry Sikorski

There is always, always, always something to be thankful for.

You don't just stumble into the future; you create your own future.

– Roger Smith

Life is too short to be little.

– Benjamin Disraeli

Do not go where the path may lead, go instead where there is no path and leave a trail.

– Ralph Waldo Emerson

Success seems to be largely a matter of hanging on after others have let go.

– William Feather

This one step, choosing a goal and sticking to it, changes everything.

– Scott Reed

Flaming enthusiasm, backed up by a horse sense and persistence, is the quality that most frequently makes for success.

– Dale Carnegie

If at first you don't succeed, skydiving is not for you.

Never confuse a single defeat with a final defeat.

– F. Scott Fitzgerald

You cannot have any success unless you can accept failure.

– George Cukor

There is no failure only feedback.

– Robert Allen

No dreamer is ever too small; no dream is ever too big.

Believing in yourself is an endless destination. Believing you have failed is the end of the journey.

Without goals and a plan to reach them, you are like a ship that has set sail with no destination.

– Fitzhugh Dodson

Consider the postage stamp: its usefulness consists of sticking to one thing until it gets there.

– Josh Billings

A thousand mile journey begins with one step.

– Lao Tsu

Expect to succeed even before you start. All winners, no matter what their game, start with the expectations that they are going to succeed. Winners say, "I want to do this and I CAN do this", not "I would like to do this, but I don't think I can".

– Denis Waitley

Goals: There is no telling what you can do when you get inspired by them. There is no telling what you can do when you believe in them. There is no telling what will happen when you act upon them.

– Jim Rohn

Aim for the top, for there is plenty of room up there. There are so few at the top it is almost lonely there.

Failure? I never encountered it. All I ever met were temporary setbacks.

– Dottie Walters

Some people dream of success, while others wake up and work hard at it!

The closer one gets to the top, the more one finds that there is no top.

– Nancy Barcus

May the pain you have known and the conflict you have experienced give you the strength to walk through life facing each new situation with courage and optimism.

You must have long-term goals to keep you from being frustrated by short-term failures.

– Charles C. Noble

The future belongs to those who believe in the beauty of their dreams.

– Elanor Roosevelt

You are successful the moment you start moving toward a worthwhile goal.

– Charles Carlson

Never give up on what you really want to do. The person with big dreams is more powerful than the one with all of the facts.
– Quote from Life's Little Instruction Book

What you get by achieving your goals is not as important as what you become by achieving your goals.
– Zig Ziglar

Never underestimate the potential and power of the human spirit.

Learn to listen. Opportunity sometimes knocks very softly.

Great minds have purpose, while others just have wishes.

– Washington Irving

Our goals can only be reached through a vehicle of a plan, in which we must fervently believe, and upon which we must vigorously act. There is no other route to success.

– Stephen A. Brennan

If I have correct goals and I keep pursuing them the best way I know how, everything falls into line. If I do the right thing, I am going to succeed.

– Dan Dierdorf

From a certain point onward there is no longer any turning back. That is the point that must be reached.
— Franz Kafka

Decide what you want, and decide what you are willing to exchange for it. Establish your priorities and go to work.
— H.L. Hunt

Nothing can stop the man with the right mental attitude from achieving his goal; nothing on earth can help the man with the wrong mental attitude.
— Thomas Jefferson

My philosophy in life is this: if we make up our mind what we are going to make of our lives, then work hard toward that goal, we never lose — somehow we win out.
— Ronald Reagan

By recording your dreams and goals on paper, you set in motion the process of becoming the person you most want to be.
– Mark Victor Hansen

Begin with the end in mind.

– Stephen Covy

Opportunity does not knock; it presents itself when you beat down the door.

– Kyle Chandler

Everyone has a fair turn to be as great as he pleases.

– Jeremy Collier

An empowered organization is one in which individuals have the knowledge, skill, desire, and opportunity to personally succeed in a way that leads to organizational success.
– Stephen Covy

The man who succeeds is the one who seizes the moment.

Goals that are not written down are just wishes.

Set your goals high enough to inspire you and low enough to encourage you.

You'll never achieve your dreams if they don't become goals.

If a person gets his attitude towards money straight, it will straighten out almost every other area in his life.

– Billy Graham

Ability is what you are capable of doing. Motivation determines what you do. Attitude determines how well you do it.

– Lou Holtz

Only those who dare to fail greatly can ever achieve greatly.

– Robert Francis Kennedy

It is time for us all to stand and cheer for the do'er, the achiever – the one who recognizes the challenge and does something about it.

– Vince Lombardi

Someone has defined genius as intensity of purpose: the ability to do, the patience to wait. Put these together and you have achievement.

– Leo J. Muir

Achievement is largely the product of steadily raising one's levels of aspirations and expectations.

Do not let what you cannot do interfere with what you can do.

– John Wooden

Opportunity often comes disguised in the form of misfortune or temporary defeat.

It still holds true that man is most uniquely human when he turns obstacles into opportunities.

– Eric Hoffer

Let your heart soar as high as it will. Refuse to be average.

– A.W. Tozer

Challenge yourself all the days of your life.

The more you seek security, the less of it you have. The more you seek opportunity, the more likely it will be that you will achieve the security you desire.

– Brian Tracy

Success is a journey, not a destination.

– Ben Sweetland

What seems impossible one minute, through faith, becomes possible the next.

– Norman Vincent Peale

Desire is the key to motivation, but it's the determination and commitment to an unrelenting pursuit of your goal, a commiment to excellence, that will enable you to attain the success you seek.

– Marrio Andretti

Success is not permanent, neither is failure.

— Dell Crossword

Determination is the wake up call to the human will.

— Anthony Robbins

There is no limit to what a man can achieve if he so believes this.

— Thomas J. Vilord

Unless you are willing to try, fail miserable, and try again, success won't happen.

— Phillip Adams

Act as though it is impossible
to fail.

An unfailing success plan: at each
day's end, write down the six most
important things to do tomorrow;
number them in order of
importance, and DO them.
No planning will work unless
we take action.

The more goals you set,
the more goals you get.

-Mark Victor Hansen

Man is always more than he can
know of himself; consequently, his
accomplishments, time and again,
will come as a surprise to him.

– Golo Mann

Trust yourself. Create the kind of person that you will be happy with all your life. Make the most of yourself by fanning the tiny inner sparks of possibility into flames of achievement.

– Foster C. McClellan

Failure is a success if we learn from it.

– Malcolm Forbes

The truth of the matter is that there is nothing you can't accomplish if you clearly decide what it is that you are absolutely committed to achieving, you are willing to take massive action, and you continue to change your approach until you achieve what you want, using whatever life gives you along the way.

– Anthony Robbins

For every problem there is an opportunity.

The will to win, the desire to succeed, the urge to reach your full potential...these are the keys that will unlock the door to personal excellence.
— Eddie Robinson

The harder you fall, the higher you bounce.

Nothing splendid has ever been achieved except by those who dared to believe that something inside them was superior to circumstances.
— Bruce Barton

If God shuts one door, another door opens.

– Irish Proverb

Our reach should exceed our grasp.

We must leave our mark on our life while we have it in our power.

– Isak Dinesen

If you want to succeed and prepare to do so, you WILL achieve your dreams.

We all have the gift of unlimited potential.

God's gifts put man's best dreams to shame.

– Elizabeth Barrett Browning

The key to will power is want power. People who want something bad enough can usually find the will power to achieve.

Joy is when anticipation meets action.

My will shall shape my future. Whether I fail or succeed shall be no man's doing but my own. I am the force; I can clear any obstacle before me, or I can be lost in a maze. My choice, my responsibility, win or lose, only I hold the key to my destiny.

– Elaine Maxwell

Believing that you can is half the battle.

Within us are the seeds of triumph or defeat.
Which seeds will you plant?

– Longfellow

Choose your dreams and leave your doubts behind.

Embrace life, have confidence in yourself, take action.

Your thoughts become your words. Your words become your actions. Your actions become your habits. Your habits become your character. Your character becomes your destiny.

Take a moment to reflect and recharge; its time well spent.

Seek not outside yourself for success lies within.

– Mary Lou Cook

Without continual growth and progress, such words as improvement, achievement, and success have no meaning.

– Benjamin Franklin

Every great achievement was once considered impossible.

Nothing is as real as a dream. Have the courage to reach for it.

You are on the road to success when you realize that failure is only a detour.

Never give up on a dream just because of the time it will take to accomplish it. The time will pass anyway.

Happy are those who dream dreams and are willing to pay the price to make them come true.

Success is determined by those who prove the impossible to be possible.

– James W. Pence

Success is the sum of small efforts repeated day in and day out.

– Robert Collier

Try not to become just a man of success, but rather try to become a man of value.

– Albert Einstein

Great work is done by people who are not afraid to be great.

– Fernando Flores

If you want a thing done well, do it yourself.

– Napoleon Bonaparte

In order to attain the impossible, one must attempt the impossible.

– Miguel de Cervantes

Hunker down!

– Steve Johnson

Whatever you are, be a good one.

– Abraham Lincoln

The only real failure is the one from which we learn nothing.

– John Powell

Difficulties mastered are opportunities won.

– Winston Churchill

I believe that the road to pre-eminent success in any line of work is to make yourself master of that line of work.
– Andrew Carnegie

Today is the best preparation for what tomorrow may bring.

Success is not the key to happiness. Happiness is the key to success. If you love what you are doing, you will be successful.
– Herman Cain

The first step is to fill your life with positive faith that will help you through anything. The second step is to start where you are.

– Norman Vincent Peale

Tomorrow's life is too late
– live today.

– Martial

Success depends upon our previous preparations, and without such preparations there is sure to be failure.

- Confucius

Look to today. Procrastination is the art of keeping up with yesterday.

– Don Marquis

The law of culture is to let each of us become all that we are capable of becoming.

Achievement comes when you decide to live your possibilities.

Live life with a fire that can never be extinguished.

In order to succeed you must fail so you know what to do better the next time.

– Anthony D'Angelo

Stumbling is not the same as falling.

– Portuguese Proverb

If you believe you can, then you will. Have confidence in your abilities, and then follow through with them.

Tomorrow belongs to those who have vision today!

If you can command yourself, you can command the world.

– Chinese Proverb

It may seem that those who do the most, dream the most.

– Stephen Leacock

Accomplishment, like life, will prove to be a journey, not a destination.

We each build our own future. We are the architects of our own fortune.

– Appius Caecus

The greatest discovery is that a human being can alter his life by altering his attitudes of his mind.

– William James

A wise man makes more opportunities than he finds.

– Francis Bacon

The major reason for setting a goal is for what it makes of you to accomplish it. What it makes of you will always be the far greater value than what you get.
– Jim Rohn

Assert your right to make a few mistakes and learn from them. Mistakes are the lessons of wisdom.

Climb high, climb far, your goal the sky, your aim the stars.

Success is all in the mind.

As a rule, he or she that has the most information will have the greatest success in life.

– Benjamin Disraeli

Please don't nag yourself with thoughts of failure. Don't set goals far beyond your capacity to achieve. Simply do what you can do, in the best way that you know how and the Lord will accept your effort.

– Gordon B. Hinkley

Make a success of living by seeing the goal and aiming at it unswervingly.

– Cecil B. DeMille

Small opportunities are often the beginning of great enterprises.

- Demosthenes

To achieve, you must believe something and want something with all your might. Then you must be willing to commit yourself to a course.

Live everyday fully as if it were your last.

– Buddha

Above all, life should be fun.

Women will never be as successful as men because they do not have wives to advise them.

– Dick Van Dyke

I like the dreams of the future
better than the history of the past.

– Thomas Jefferson

Nothing will come of nothing;
we must dare mighty things.

– William Shakespeare

Every strike brings me closer to
the next home run.

– Babe Ruth

The key to happiness is having
dreams. The key to success is
making your dreams come true.

Success is a state of mind. If you want success, start thinking of yourself as a success!

— Dr. Joyce Brothers

History has demonstrated that the most notable winners usually encountered heart-breaking obstacles before they triumphed. They won because they refused to become discouraged by their defeat.

— B.C. Forbes

Go confidently in the direction of your dreams. Live the life you've imagined.

— Henry David Thoreau

If anyone else can do it, or make it in life, so can I.

— Thomas J. Vilord

It is not enough to have a good mind; the important thing is to use it well.
– Rene Descartes

You can't hit a home run unless you step up to the plate. You can't catch a fish if you don't put your line in the water. You can't reach your goals if you don't try.
– Kathy Seligman

There is one quality that one must possess to win, and that is definiteness of purpose, the knowledge of what one wants, and a burning desire to possess it.
– Napoleon Hill

Go as far as you can see, and when you get there you will see further.

– Orison Swett Marden

Do not let the future be held
hostage by the past.

– Neal A. Maxwell

No one knows what he can do
until he tries.

– Publilius Syrus

If one advances confidently in
the direction of his own dreams
and endeavors to live the life
that he has imagined, he will meet
with a success unexpected
in common hours.

– Henry David Thoreau

You can't hit a target you cannot
see and you cannot see a target
you do not have.

– Zig Ziglar

Each problem has in it an opportunity so powerful that it literally dwarfs the problem. The greatest success stories were created by people who recognized a problem and turned it into an opportunity.

– Joseph Sugarman

Success is willing to do what the average person is not willing to do.

It is the man who is waiting for his ship to come in that is always missing the boat.

What am I willing to sacrifice to become what I want to become?

If there is any one axiom that I have tried to live up to in attempting to become successful in business, it is the fact that I have tried to surround myself with associates that know more about business than I do. This policy has always been very successful and is still working for me.

– Monte L. Bean

The state of your life is nothing more than a reflection of your state of mind.

– Dr. Wayne W. Dyer

Always look at what you have left and what is left to come. Never look at what you have lost.

– Robert H. Schuller

If you believe you can, you probably can. If you believe you won't, you most assuredly won't. Belief is the ignition switch that gets you off the launching pad.
– Denis Waitley

Minds are like parachutes – they only function when open.

– Thomas Dewar

A great attitude does much more than turn on the lights in our worlds; it seems to magically connect us to all sorts of serendipitous opportunities that were somehow absent before we changed.

– Earl Nightingale

Happiness is not by chance, but by choice.

– Jim Rohn

Live with passion.

– Anthony Robbins

Keep on trying…each failure is one step closer to a success.

– Thomas J. Vilord

I never expect to lose. Even when I am the underdog, I still prepare a victory speech.

– H. Jackson Browne

Attitude determines altitude.

If you change anything about the way you approach selling, the thing that would make the biggest difference would be your attitude – your attitude toward your customer, your service, the benefits of your products, your employer, and yourself.

– Dan Brent Burnt

Success is not final and failure is not fatal. It is the courage to continue that counts.

– Winston Churchill

For a righteous man falls seven times and rises again.

– Proverbs 24:16

The horizon is out there somewhere if you just keep looking for it, chasing it, and working for it.

– Bob Dole

What counts is not necessarily the size of the dog in the fight, but the size of the fight in the dog.

– General Dwight Eisenhower

The most important thing is to know that you can do it.

– Robert G. Allen

The more you prospect, the more you prosper.

– Steve Johnson

Before success comes in any man's life, he is sure to meet with much temporary defeat, and perhaps some failures. When defeat overtakes a man, the easiest and most logical thing to do is to quit. That is what the majority of men do. That is why the majority is just ordinary.

– Napoleon Hill

Success doesn't come to you;
you go to it.

– Marva Collins

If you are truly flexible and go
until...there is very little you can't
accomplish in your lifetime.

– Anthony Robbins

The ultimate is not to win, but to
reach within the depths of your
capabilities and become the best
you can possibly be.

– Thomas J. Vilord

How long should you try?
Until...

It is the man's dreams and his inspiring attempt to make them come true that remain important.

– Francis Ford Coppola

I don't dream at night, I dream all day; I dream for a living.

– Steven Spielberg

Vision without action is merely a dream. Action without vision just passes time. Vision with action can change the world.

– Joel Barker

We should show our lives not as it is or how it ought to be, but only as we see it in our dreams.

– Count Leo Tolstoy

Throw back the shoulders, let the heart sing, let the eyes flash, let the mind be lifted up, look upward and say to yourself, "Nothing is impossible!!!"
– Norman Vincent Peale

Unless you have tried to do something beyond what you have already mastered, you will never grow.

– Ronald E. Osborn

The real secret to success is enthusiasm.

– Walter Chrysler

To change one's life we must start immediately and do it flamboyantly. No exceptions.

– William James

Beware when God lets loose a thinker on this planet.

– Ralph Waldo Emerson

Forget past mistakes and forget failures. Forget everything except what you are going to do now and do it.

– William Durant

It is our attitude at the end of a difficult task, which more than anything else, will affect its successful outcome.

– William James

We cannot become what we want to be by remaining what we are.

– Max Depree

Develop an attitude of gratitude, and give thanks for everything that happens to you, knowing that every step forward is a step toward achieving something bigger and better than your current situation.

— Brian Tracy

Success as I see it is a result, not a goal.

— Gustave Flaubert

A great pleasure in life is doing what people say you cannot do.

— Walter Gagehot

If you want to know your past, look into your present conditions. If you want to know your future, look into your present actions.

I have missed more than 9,000 shots in my career. I have lost almost 300 games. On 26 occasions I have been entrusted to take the game winning shot...and I missed. I have failed over and over and over again in my life and that's precisely why I succeed.

– Michael Jordan

I am not telling you that achieving success is going to be easy, I am telling you that it's going to be worth it!

– Art Williams

A person is led on the path that he truly wants to travel on.

– The Talmud

The greatest mistake you can make in your life is to be continually fearing that you will make one.

– Elbert Hubbard

You are today where your
thoughts have brought you; you
will be tomorrow where your
thoughts take you.
— James Allen

The trouble with many plans is
that they are based on the way
things are now. To be successful,
your personal plan must focus on
what you want, not what you have.
— Nido Qubein

It takes time to succeed because
success is merely the natural
reward of taking time to do
anything well.

— Joseph Ross

Life is either a daring adventure,
or nothing at all.

— Helen Keller

For with God all things are
possible.

– Mark 10:27

Nothing can add more power to
your life than concentrating all of
your energies on a limited
set of targets.

– Nido Qubein

A man is a success if he gets up in
the morning and goes to bed at
night, and in between does what
he wants to do.

– Bob Dylan

There is only one success – to be
able to spend your life in your own
way that you want.

– Christopher Morley

You can change all things for the better when you change yourself for the better.

– Jim Rohn

Aim for success, not perfection. Never give up your right to be wrong, because then you will lose your ability to learn new things and move forward in your life.

– Dr. David M. Burns

Men are born to succeed, not fail.

– Henry David Thoreau

A successful individual typically sets his next goal somewhat, but not too much above his last achievement. In this way he steadily raises his level of aspiration.

– Kurt Lewin

Whenever I hear it can't be done, I know I am close to success.

– Michael Flatley

You always pass failure on the way to success.

– Mickey Rooney

Formulate and stamp indelibly on your mind a mental picture of yourself as succeeding. Hold this picture tenaciously and never permit it to fade. Your mind will seek to develop this picture!

– Norman Vincent Peale

A minute of success pays for years of failure.

– Robert Browning

Success is to go from one failure to another with no loss of enthusiasm.

– Winston Churchill

To achieve great things, we must dream as well as act.

– Anatole France

Those who dream by day are cognizant of many things that escape those who dream only by night.

– Edgar Allen Poe

There is nothing like a dream to create the future. Utopia today, flesh and blood tomorrow.

– Victor Hugo

Your talent is God's gift to you. What you do with it is your gift back to God.

– Leo Buscaglia

Don't go through life, GROW through life.

– Eric Butterworth

I have heard it said that the first ingredient of success, the earliest spark in the dreaming youth is this: dream a great dream.

Vision is the art of seeing things that are not yet visible.

– Jonathan Swift

You must do the things you
think you cannot do.

– Elanor Roosevelt

I have had enough success for two
lifetimes. My success is talent put
together with hard work and luck.

– Kareem Abdul-Jabbar

Enthusiasm is contagious
– start an epidemic.

If at first you don't succeed, you
are running about average.

– M.H. Alderson

Most success springs from an obstacle or failure.

– Scott Adams

A desire to be in charge of our own lives, and a need for control is born in each of us. It is essential to our mental health, and our success, that we take control.
– Robert F. Bennett

The most successful men in the end are those whose success is the result of steady accretion. It is the man who carefully advances step by step, with his mind becoming wider and wider, and progressively better able to grasp any theme or situation – persevering in what he knows to be practical, and concentrating his thought upon it. This is the man who is bound to succeed in the greatest degree.

– Alexander Graham Bell

One must have strategies to execute dreams.

The difference between success and mediocrity is all in the way you think.

The truth is that all of us can attain the greatest success and happiness possible in this life whenever we use our native capacities to its greatest extent.
– Smiley Blanton

Nature gave us two ends: one to sit on and one to think with. Ever since then, man's success or failure has been dependent on the one he used most.
– Robert Albert Bloch.

You are never too old to set
another goal or to dream a
new dream.

– Les Brown

Never let your failures go to
your heart or your successes
go to your head.

The first and most important step
toward success is the feeling that
we can succeed.

– Nelson Boswell

Studies indicate that the one quality
all successful people have is persistence.
They are willing to spend more time
accomplishing a task and to persevere in the
face of many difficult odds. There is a very
positive relationship between people's
ability to accomplish any task and the time
they are willing to spend on it.

– Dr. Joyce Brothers

It takes twenty years to make an overnight success.

– Eddie Cantor

Nobody succeeds beyond his or her wildest expectations unless he or she begins with some wild expectations.

– Ralph Charell

The great successful men of the world have used their imagination. They think ahead and create their mental picture in all its details and steadily building upon it.

– Robert J. Collier

If I had permitted my failures, or what seemed to me at the time a lack of success, to discourage me, I cannot see any way in which I would have ever made progress.

– Calvin Coolidge

I don't know the key to success, but the key to failure is trying to please everybody.

– Bill Cosby

Failure is instructive. The person who really thinks, learns just as much from his failures as he does from his successes.

– John Dewey

The secret to success in life is for a man to be ready for his opportunity when it comes.

– Benjamin Disraeli

To succeed you need to find something to hold onto, something to motivate you, and something to inspire you.

– Tony Dorsett

To dream anything you want to dream, that is the beauty of the human mind. To do anything that you want to do, that is the strength of the human will. To trust yourself to test your limits, that is the courage to succeed.
— Bernard Edmunds

Persistent people begin their success where others end in failure.

— Edward Eggleston

One sound idea is all that you need to achieve success.

— Napoleon Hill

The greatest happiness is to transform your feelings into actions.

— Madame de Stael

Working hard overcomes a whole lot of other obstacles. You can have unbelievable intelligence, you can have connections, and you can have opportunities fall out of the sky. But in the end, hard work is the true, enduring characteristic of successful people.

– Marsha Evans

It is only as we develop others that we permanently succeed.

– Harvey Samuel Firestone

There is no point at which you can say, "Well I am successful now, I might as well relax".

– Carrie Fisher

Coming together is the beginning.
Keeping together is progress.
Working together is success.

– Henry Ford

Champions know that success is
inevitable, that there is no such
thing as failure, only feedback.
They know that the best way to
forecast the future is to create it.
– Michael J. Gelb

Losers visualize the penalties of
failure; winners visualize the
rewards of success.

– William S. Gilbert

Success gravitates to those who
are perceived to be successful.
Regardless of how you feel
within, you must emanate success
if you want to be a success.

Patience, persistence, and perspiration make an unbeatable combination for success.

– Napoleon Hill

Success isn't magic or hocus-pocus – its simply learning how to focus.

– Jack Canfield

Of course we all have our limits, but how can you possibly find your boundaries unless you explore as far and as wide as you possibly can? I would rather fail at an attempt at something new and uncharted, than safely succeed in a repeat of something I have already done.

– A.E. Hotchner

A man achieves according to what he believes.

It is the man who has done nothing that says nothing can be done.

If you have talent and you work long and hard at it, anything in the world can be yours.

The man who believes he can do it is probably right, and so is the man who says he can't.

An optimist expects his dreams to come true. A pessimist expects his nightmares to come true.

The secret of success is this: there is no secret to success.

– Elbert Hubbard

The road to success is always under construction.

There is plenty of room at the top, but there is no room to sit down.

A successful man is one who earns more than his wife can spend; a successful woman is one who marries such a man.

The secret of success is to never let down and never let up.

None of the secrets of success will work unless you do.

Our belief at the beginning of a doubtful undertaking is the one thing that assures the successful outcome of any venture.
– William James

Success comes in can's.
Failures come in cant's.

Behind every successful man
stands a surprised mother-in-law.

– Hubert H. Humphrey

There are no speed limits on the
road to success.

– David W. Johnson

The men who try to do something
and fail are infinitely better than
those who do nothing and succeed.

– Lloyd Jones

Character cannot be developed in ease and quiet. Only through experience, trial, and suffering can the soul be strengthened, vision cleared, ambition inspired, and success achieved.
– Helen Keller

Champions believe in themselves, even if no one else does.

Get a good idea and stay with it. Dog it, and stay with it until it's done right.

– Walt Disney

An inventor fails 999 times and, and if he succeeds once, he's victorious. He treats his failures as practice shots.

– Charles Franklin Kettering

You've got to say, "I think that if I keep working at this and want it badly enough, I can have it." It's called perseverance.

- Lee Iacocca

Intelligence without ambition is like a bird without wings.

- C. Archie Danielson

Yes, risk taking is inherently failure-prone. Otherwise it would be called sure-thing taking.

- Tim McMahon

I wasn't afraid to fail. Something good always comes out of failure.

- Anne Baxter

Just like a turtle, we only make progress if we stick our neck out.

- James Bryant Conant

Learn something new every single day. You will never get old if you do.

- Lois Bey

The desire of knowledge, like the thirst of riches, increases ever with the acquisition of it.

- Laurence Sterne

Great minds have purposes, others have wishes. Little minds are tamed and subdued by misfortune, but great minds rise above them.

- Washington Irving

Those who are quite satisfied sit still and do nothing; those who are not quite satisfied are the sole benefactors of the world.

- Walter Savage Landor

The one thing worse than a quitter is the person who is afraid to begin.

There is no great success without great commitment.

We make a living by what we get, but we make a life by what we give.

- Winston Churchill

Doing your best is more important than being the best.

The difference between a successful person and the others is not a lack of strength and not a lack of knowledge, but a lack of will.
- Vince Lombardi

Between each down and setting sun, set aside some time for fun.

An obstacle may be either a stepping-stone or a stumbling block.

Give me a lever long enough, and a prop strong enough and I can single-handedly move the world.

– Archimedes

What we do today, right now, will have an accumulated effect on all of our tomorrows.

- Alexandra Stoddard

Wisdom is knowing what to do next; virtue is doing it.

Our imagination is the only limit to what we can hope to have in the future.

- Charles Kettering

Take heed: you do not find
what you do not seek.

- English Proverb

Failing to plan is planning
to fail.

- Effie Jones

Once a man has made a commitment to a way of life, he puts the greatest
strength in the world behind him. It's something we call heart power.
Once a man has made this commitment, nothing will stop him
short of success.

- Vince Lombardi

I will persist until I succeed. Always will I take another step and if that is of no avail, I will take another, and yet another. In truth, one step at a time is not too difficult. I know that small attempts repeated will complete any undertaking.

- Og Mandino

Many a man has finally succeeded only because he has failed after repeated efforts. If he had never met defeat, he would never have known any great victory.

- Orison Swett Marden

Youth is not enough. Love is not enough. Success is not enough. And if we could ever achieve it, enough would not be enough.

- Mignon McLaughlin

Courage changes things for the better. With courage, you can stay with something long enough to succeed at it, realizing that it usually takes two, three, or four times as long to succeed as you thought or hoped.

- Earl Nightingale

The intelligent man is one who has successfully fulfilled many accomplishments, and is still willing to learn more.

- Ed Parker

There are no secrets to success. It is the result of preparation, hard work, and learning from failure.

- Colin Powell

Nothing great will ever be achieved without great men, and men are only great if they are determined to be so.

- Charles de Gaulle

You can do what you want to do, and sometimes you can do it even better than you thought you could.

- Jimmy Carter

A failure establishes only this: that our determination to succeed was not strong enough.

- John Christian Boves

The price of success is hard work, dedicated to the job at hand, and the determination that whether we win or lose, we have applied the best of ourselves to the task at hand.
- Vince Lombardi

If you want to be successful, it's just this simple: know what you are doing, love what you are doing, and believe in what you are doing.

- Will Rogers

Never mind what others do; do better than yourself, beat your own record each and everyday, and you are a success.

- William Boetcker

There is scarcely an instance of a man who has made a fortune by speculation, and kept it.

– Andrew Carnegie

If you have nothing else to do, look at yourself and see if there isn't something close at hand that you can improve. It may make you wealthy, although it is more likely it will make you happy.

– George Matthew Adams

People rarely succeed unless they have fun in what they are doing.

– Dale Carnegie

Success is never wondering what if…

- Karrie Huffman

The greatest thing about a man is his ability to transcend himself, his environment, and to be what he dreams of being.

– Tully C. Knoles

All of our dreams can come true if we have the courage to pursue them.

– Walt Disney

It is a fabulous country, the only fabulous country; it is the only place where miracles not only happen, but they happen all of the time.

- Thomas Wolf

"I can't do it" never accomplished anything; "I will try" has performed miracles.

– George P. Burnham

The great accomplishments of man have resulted from the transmission of ideas, into enthusiasm, into actions.

– Thomas J. Watson

Throughout the centuries there have been men who took the first steps down new roads armed with nothing but their own vision.

– Ayn Rand

Start by doing what is necessary, then what is possible, and suddenly you are doing the impossible.

– Francis of Assisi

Don't limit yourself. Many people limit themselves to what they think they can do. You can go as far as your mind lets you. What you believe, you can achieve!

– Mary Kay Ash

The only thing ever achieved in life without effort is failure.

There are two ways of meeting difficulties: you can alter the difficulties, or you can alter yourself to meet the difficulties.

– Phyllis Bottoms

Believe in yourself! Have faith in your abilities! Without a humble, but reasonable confidence in your own powers, you cannot be successful or happy.
— Norman Vincent Peale

Remove failure as an option.

— Joan Lunden

Far better is it to dare mighty things to win glorious triumphs, even though checkered with failure, than to make rank with those poor spirits who neither enjoy much nor suffer much, because they live in the gray twilight that knows not victory or defeat.
— Theodore Roosevelt

Men succeed when they realize that their failures are the preparation for their victories.

— Ralph Waldo Emerson

There isn't a person anywhere that isn't capable of doing more than he thinks he can.

— Henry Ford

Never stand begging for something that you have the power to earn.

— Miguel de Cervantes

To succeed it is necessary to accept the world as it is and rise above it.

— Michael Korda

The individual activity of one man with a backbone will do more than a thousand men with a mere wish bone.

– William Boetcke

Failure is just an opportunity to begin again...this time more wisely.

What would you attempt if you knew you could not fail?

– Anthony Robbins

If you are not going to think big, don't bother thinking at all.

– Thomas J. Vilord

There is real magic in enthusiasm. It spells the difference between mediocrity and accomplishment.

In the end, the size of a man's accomplishments can best be measured by the size of their heart.

A mediocre idea that generates enthusiasm will go farther than a great idea that inspires no one.

– Mary Kay Ashe

A man can succeed at almost anything for which he has unlimited enthusiasm.

– Charles Schwab

A man's dreams are an index to his greatness.

– Zadok Rabinowitz

Nothing is hopeless; we must hope for everything.

– Madeline L'Engle

When you come to the edge of all that you know, you must believe on one of two things: there will be earth upon which to stand, or you will be given wings to fly.

What we must decide is how we are valuable, rather than how valuable we are.

- F. Scott Fitzgerald

You can often measure a man
by the size of his dreams.

– Robert H. Schuller

The uncommon man is merely
the common man thinking and
dreaming of success in larger
terms and in more
fruitful areas.

– Melvin Powers

The poorest man in the world
is not a man without a cent
to his name, but it's the man
who does not have a dream.

The recipe of success is to study
while others are sleeping, work
while others are loafing, prepare
while others are playing, and
dream while others are wishing.

– William A. Ward

Success consists of getting up just one more time than you fall.

– Oliver Goldsmith

To have more than you've got, become more than you are.

– Jim Rohn

I still say that I am a little different because success to me is not having the most money, or having the biggest car or the biggest house. Success is just being happy.

– Herschel Walker

The future is purchased by what you do in the present.

Success is doing what you want
to do, when you want,
with whomever you want,
as much as you want.

– Anthony Robbins

The only way to excellence is
to consistently improve yourself
every single day.

– Thomas J. Vilord

Enthusiasm is the vital element
toward the individual success of
every man or woman.

– Conrad Hilton

I want to seize fate by the throat.

– Ludwig van Beethoven

The very essence of leadership is having vision.

– Father Theodore Hesburg

The successful man will profit from his mistakes and try again in a different way.

– Dale Carnegie

Success comes to those who make it happen, not those who let it happen.

Some of my fondest memories in sports were a result of failure, injuries, setbacks, and mistakes. I learned far more about myself and gained more character in those difficult times than I ever did when success came early.

– Peter Vidmar

In the marathon of life, success calls for dedication to the goal, perseverance, compassion for my fellow man, and faith in God.

– John A. Kelley.

Wherever you see a successful business, someone once made courageous decision.

– Peter Drucker

Courage is daring to take the first step, or a different path. It is the decision to place your dreams above your fears.

The currents that determine our dreams and shape our lives, flow from the attitudes that we nurture everyday.

Happiness, wealth, and success are the byproducts of goal setting; they cannot be the goals themselves.

– Denis Waitley

Triumph is just a little "umph" added to try.

This is the beginning of a new day. You have been given this day to use as you will. You can waste it, or use it for good. What you do today is important because you are exchanging a day of your life for it.

The happiness of your life depends on the quality of your thoughts.

Its kind of fun to do the impossible.

– Walt Disney

Put your goals in writing. If you can't put it on a sheet of paper, you probably can't do what it takes to achieve the goal.

Failure is the path of least PERSISTENCE.

Hard work is the yeast that raises the dough.

Goals are like the stars:
they are always there.
Adversity is like the clouds:
they are temporary and will
move on. Keep your eyes
on the stars.

If you want your dreams
to come true,
don't oversleep.

God's retirement plan is
out of this world.

Our lives are not determined by what
happens to us, but how we react to what
happens; not what life brings to us, but
the attitude that we bring to life. A positive attitude causes a chain reaction of
positive thoughts, events and outcomes.
It is a catalyst...a spark that creates
extraordinary results.

Past failures are guideposts for future success.

We cannot change yesterday, we can only make the most of today and look with hope toward tomorrow.

A positive attitude is a powerful force…it can't be stopped.

The one who lacks the courage to start has already finished.

We are what and where we are because we have first imagined it.

– Donald Curtis

A quitter never wins and a winner never quits.

The highest courage is to dare to be yourself in the face of adversity. Choosing right over wrong, ethics over convenience, and truth over popularity. These are the choices that measure your life. Travel the path of integrity without looking back, for there will never be a wrong time to do the right thing.

The reward for work well done is the opportunity to do more.

There are two ways to live your life. One is believing that nothing is a miracle, and the other is believing that everything is a miracle.

If you aren't fired up with enthusiasm, you'll be fired with enthusiasm.

Most of us are just as happy as we make up our minds to be.

- Abraham Lincoln

The darkest hour of any man's life is when he sits down to plan how to get money without earning it.

– Horace Greeley

It takes a single idea and a single action to move the world.

You can do it if you put your mind to it.

A leader's job is to look into the future and see the organization not as it is, but as it can become.

Our life is what our thoughts make it. Do the best that you can, where you are, with what you have.

– Marcus Aurelius

Happiness doesn't depend on what we have, but it does depend on how we feel toward what we have. We can be happy with little and miserable with much.

- William Dempster Hoard

Attitude is a little thing that makes a big difference.

A bump in the road is either an obstacle to be fought, or an opportunity to be enjoyed… it's all up to you.

Great customer service is still the best way to beat the pants off the competition.

Our destiny is shaped by our thoughts and our actions. We cannot direct the wind, but we can adjust the sails.

Success is the person who year after year, reaches the highest limits in his field.

– Sparky Anderson

Out of respect of things I was never destined to do, I have learned that my strengths are a result of my weaknesses, my success is due to my failures, and my style is directly related to my limitations.

– Billy Joel

The most absurd and reckless aspirations have sometimes led to extraordinary success.

You must think of failure and defeat as the spring boards to new achievements, and to the next level of accomplishment.

– Les Brown

Even a mistake may turn out to be the one thing necessary to a worthwhile achievement.

– Henry Ford

Cherish your visions and your dreams, as they are the children of your soul, and the blueprints of your ultimate achievements.

– Napoleon Hill

Hope is not a dream, but a way of making dreams become reality.

– Cardinal Sueneus

So many or our dreams at first seem impossible, then they seem improbable, and then, when we summon the will, they soon become inevitable.

– Christopher Reeve

America is the greatest country in the world. You can be anything you want to be within the laws of God and man. You can make your dreams come true if you work hard, stay focused on your goal, and give back to the community that supports you.

– R. David Thomas

Dreams do come true if we only wish hard enough. You can have anything in life if you will sacrifice everything else for it.

– Sir James M. Barrie

Action, to be effective, must be directed to clearly conceived ends.

– J. Nehru

The moment of enlightenment is when a person's dreams of possibilities become images of probabilities.

– Vic Bruden

Don't let failure get you down. Babe Ruth struck out 1,300 times.

– Lou Holtz

When defeat comes, accept it as a signal that your plans are not sound. Rebuild those plans and set sail once more toward your coveted goal.

– Napoleon Hill

Ideas are the beginning of all achievement.

– Bruce Lee

You can do what you what to do, accomplish what you want to accomplish, attain any reasonable objective you may have in mind, not all of a sudden, perhaps not in one swift and sweeping act of achievement, but you can do it gradually, day by day, and play by play, if you want to do it, if you work to do it, over a sufficiently long period of time.

– William E. Holler

Success has always been easy to measure. It's the distance between one's origins and one's final achievement.
— Michael Korda

May your future be worthy of your dreams.

— Barbara Bush

I have had dreams and I have had nightmares.
I overcame my nightmares because of
my dreams.

— Jonas Salk

I have learned that we cannot forget or throw away our past, but we must not let our past to control us either. We must learn and grow from our past failures, disappointments, and painful experiences.
Reset our goals and priorities and move forward. Start today by untying the knots that are limiting you.

– Ty Howard

Leaders are not born; they are made. And they are made just like anything else - through hard work. and that is the price we'll have to pay to achieve any goal.

– Vince Lomnbardi

Never give up. If you want to be something, be conceited about it. Give yourself a chance. Never say that you are not good for that will never get you anywhere. Set high goals. That is what life is all about.

– Mike McLaren

Success is the progressive realization of predetermined, worthwhile, personal goals.

– Paul Meyer

Let me tell you the secret that has led me to my goal: my strength lies solely in my tenacity.

– Louis Pasteur

Discipline is the bridge between goals and accomplishment.

– Jim Rohn

Happiness is not in the mere possession of money. It lies in the joy of achievement and in the thrill of creative effort.

– Franklin Delano Roosevelt

The goal of every married couple indeed and every Christian home should be to make Christ the head, the Counselor, and the Guide.

– Paul Sadler

Think little goals and expect little achievements. Think big goals and win big success.

– David Joseph Schwartz

Dream no small dreams, for they have no power to stir the souls of men.

– Victor Hugo

When we are motivated by goals that have deep meaning, by dreams that need completion, by pure love that needs expressing, it is then when we truly live.

– Greg Anderson

Every great work, every great accomplishment, has been brought into manifestation through holding to the vision, and often comes apparent and temporary failure and discouragement just before the big achievement.

– Florence Scovel Shinn

All successful men and women are big dreamers. They imagine what their future could be, ideal in every respect, and then they work everyday toward their distant vision, goal, and purpose!

– Brian Tracy

The man who gives up accomplishes nothing and is only a hindrance. The man who does not give up can move mountains.

- Ernest Hello

The achievement of your goal is assured the moment you commit yourself to it!

– Mark R. Douglas

Nothing stops a man who desires to achieve. Every obstacle is simply a course to develop his achievement muscles. It's a strengthening of his powers toward accomplishment.

– Eric Butterworth

Great things are completed by talented people who believe they will accomplish them.

– Warren G. Bennis

The reason most people never reach their goals is because they do not define them, or even seriously consider them as believable or achievable. Winners can tell you where they are going, what they plan to do along the way, and who will be sharing the adventure with them.

– Denis Waitley

There is no finer sensation in life than that which comes with victory over one's self. Go forward to a goal of inward achievement, brushing aside all of your old internal enemies as you advance.

– Vash Young

If you want to reach a goal, you must see yourself reaching it in your own mind before you actually arrive at your goal.

– Zig Ziglar

You can have anything you want if you want it badly enough. You can be anything you want to be, do anything you set out to accomplish if you hold to that desire with singleness of purpose.

– William Adams

Optimism is essential to achievement and it is also the foundation of courage and true progress.

– Lloyd Alexander

For a man to achieve all that is demanded of him, he must regard himself as greater than he is.

– Johann Wolfgang von Goethe

He who labors diligently need never despair, for all things are accomplished by diligence and labor.

– Menander

Lord, grant that I might always desire more than I can accomplish.

– Michelangelo

The game of life is to come up a winner, to be a success, and to achieve what you set out to do.

– Richard Nixon

If you want to be successful, find someone who has achieved the results you want, and copy what they do, and you'll achieve similar results.

– Anthony Robbins

To achieve the impossible, it is precisely the unthinkable that must be thought.

– Tom Robbins

Every achiever that I have ever met says, "My life turned around when I began to believe in me."

– Robert H. Schuller

There are two things to aim at in life: first, to get what you want and second is to enjoy it. Only the wisest of mankind achieve the second.

– Logan Pearsall Smith

Success is achieved and maintained by those who try, and keep trying, for there is nothing to lose by trying and a great deal to gain if successful. By all means TRY! Do it NOW!!!

– W. Clement Stone

The roots of true achievement lie in the will to become the best that you can become.

– Harold Taylor

Use failures as stepping-stones to deeper understanding and greater achievement.

Outstanding leaders go out of their way to boost the self-esteem of their personnel. If people believe in themselves, it is amazing at what they can accomplish.

– Sam Walton

If you can imagine it, you can achieve it; if you can dream it, you can become it.

– William Arthur Ward

One can choose to go back toward safety or forward toward growth. Growth must be chosen again and again; fear must be overcome again and again.

– Abraham Maslow

The real risk is doing nothing.

– Denis Waitley

Your current situation is no indication of your ultimate potential!

– Anthony Robbins

What you can do, or dream you can, begin it. Boldness has genius, power, and magic in it.

– Johann Wolfgang von Goethe

What a man thinks of himself is what determines, or rather indicates his fate.

– Henry David Thoreau

If we don't change, we don't grow. If we don't grow, we aren't really living.

– Gail Sheehy

No life ever grows great until it is focused, dedicated, and disciplined.

– Henry Emerson Forsdick

Dream pass into the reality of action. From this action comes the dream again, and this produces the highest form of living.

– Anais Nin

In adversity keep motivated, because often the best results come from difficulties.

It's always too soon to quit.

First thing every morning before you arise out of bed, say out loud three times "I believe I can."

The belief that becomes truth for me... is that which allows me the best use of my strength, the best means of putting my virtues into action.

– Andre Gide

Never use the word "impossible". Throw it into the verbal waste bucket.

When you expect the best, you release a force in your mind that tends to bring out the best in you.

Our real problem is not our strength today; it is rather the vital necessity of action today to ensure our strength tomorrow.

– Calvin Coolidge

If you think you can win, you can win. Faith is necessary for victory.

– William Hazlitt

Time is our most valuable asset, yet we tend to waste it, kill it, and spend it rather than invest it.

– Jim Rohn

Set too many goals and keep adding more goals. Goals have a tendency to be realized all at once.

– Mark Victor Hansen

Success is directly proportional to effort.

Nothing is so contagious as enthusiasm; it is the genius of sincerity, and the truth accomplishes nothing without it.

Opportunities are multiplied as they are seized.

Plan to succeed or you have planned to fail.

There are risks and costs to a plan of action, but they are far less than the long-term risks and costs of comfortable inactions.

Dreams come true for those who work while they dream.

There are those who see an opportunity, and those who SEIZE an opportunity.

The future belongs to those who see possibilities before they become obvious.

When facing a difficult task, act as if you cannot fail.

Great people are created by great mistakes that are learned from, not from great successes that are gloated upon.

– Elmer Clark

Motivation is what gets you started; habit is what keeps you going.

– Jim Ryun

Those who want to succeed will find a way; those who don't will find an excuse.

– Leo Aguila

It's amazing what ordinary people can do if they set out with preconceived notions.

– Charles F. Kettering

If you mess up and learn nothing, it's a mistake. If you mess up and learn something, it's an experience.

– Mark McFadden

No matter how small, acknowledge the achievement.

– Greg Henry Quinn

People who are afraid to fail can never experience the joys of success.

Procrastination is the seed of self-destruction.

– Matthew Burton

Except and expect positive things, and that is what you will receive.

– Lori Hard

Thoughts are like a flame: small thoughts produce small heat, and big thoughts make an inferno.

– Jim Lu

Success is not all about money. It's about having the resources and the ability to live the life that you have personally dreamed of.
— Pete Zafra

If you don't think everyday is a great day, try going without one.

— Jim Evans

The body achieves what the mind believes.

To learn, you have to listen. To improve, you have to try.

— Thomas Jefferson

Even if something has just a one percent chance of success, success boils down to how fast you exhaust your ninety-nine failures.

One of the most important principles of success is developing the habit of going the extra mile.

– Napoleon Hill

The meeting of preparation with opportunity generates the offspring we call luck.

– Anthony Robbins

The philosophy of the rich versus the poor is this: The rich invest their money and spends what is left; the poor spends their money and invest what is left.

– Jim Rohn

Perfection is our goal;
excellence will be tolerated.

Vision plus desire equals reality.

If you can dream it, you can do it.
Your limits are all within yourself.

– Brian Tracy

We must have courage to bet on
our ideas, take the calculated risk,
and take action!

– Martin Brown

Impossibility is an opinion, not a fact.

A winner never stops trying.

– Tom Landry

Life is a state of mind; imagine the one that you want, and then create it.

The secret to success is to do common things uncommonly well.

– John D. Rockefeller, Sr.

The surest way not to fail is to be determined to succeed.

Winners must have two things: definite goals, and a burning desire to achieve them.

– Brad Burden

I don't know what my future holds, but I do know who holds my future.

The three P's of success: Passion, Persistence, and Patience.

– Doug Bronson

Better is not something you wish, it is something you become.

– Jim Rohn

He has achieved success if he has lived well, laughed often, and loved much.

– Bessie Stanley

True success is overcoming the fear of being unsuccessful.

– Paul Sweeney

If you are successful, you may win false friends and true enemies. Succeed anyway.

– Mother Theresa

What is success? I think it is a mixture of having a flair for the thing that you are doing; knowing that it is not enough, that you must have hard work and a certain sense of purpose.
– Margaret Thatcher

No one lives long enough to learn everything they need to learn starting from scratch. To be successful, we absolutely, positively have to find people who have already paid the price to learn the things that we need to learn to achieve our goals.

– Brian Tracy

Some of the best lessons we ever learn are learned from past mistakes. The error of the past is the wisdom and success of the future.
– Dr. Dale Turner

If you can't find the key to success, pick the lock.

Yesterday's failures are today's seeds that must be diligently planted to be able to abundantly harvest tomorrow's success.

Some people succeed because they are destined to, but most people succeed because they are determined to.

Forget about the consequences of failure. Failure is only a temporary change in direction to set you straight for your next success.
– Denis Waitley

You don't pay the price for success. You enjoy the price for success.

– Zig Ziglar

It takes a person who is wide-awake to make his dream come true.

– Roger Ward Babson

You gotta have a dream! If you don't have a dream how are you gonna make a dream come true?

– Oscar Hammerstein, II

What distinguishes us from one another is our dreams, and what we do to make them come about.

– Joseph Epstein

Within our dreams and aspirations we find our opportunities.

You must see your goals clearly and specifically before you can set out for them. Hold them in your mind until they become second nature.

– Les Brown

Set your goals high and don't stop until you get there.

- Bo Jackson

Work like you don't need the money, love like you've never been hurt, and dance like nobody is watching.

– Mark Twain

<u>Author Biography</u>

Thomas J. Vilord is a licensed Financial Advisor with Morgan Stanley in the Cherry Hill, New Jersey office. Mr. Vilord has been serving clients in the New Jersey and Philadelphia area for the past six years.

In addition to motivational speaking, Mr. Vilord is an active speaker on investments and financial planning. To book a speaking engagement, please call 1-800-676-2201, or to reach Mr. Vilord directly, call

856-489-5847

Order Form for Additional Books

Quantity_____ @ $10.99   Total_____
Add $2.00 for shipping and handling for
the first book and $.50 for each additional book.   _____
                                        Grand Total _____
Telephone Orders: Call 856-371-0146. Have your credit card ready.

Check Orders: Send your order along with check or money order to:
Garden State Publishing
100 Springdale Road, A3
PMB# 207
Cherry Hill, NJ 08003
Name _____
Address _____
City _____State_____ Zip_____
Telephone Number _____

Or order by credit card:
Visa _____ Master Card _____
Card Number_____
Name on Card_____ Exp. Date _____

If you are not happy with your order, you may return it for a full refund at any time...
no questions asked!